· PEOPLES of NORTH AMERICA ·

Apache

— VALERIE BODDEN —

CREATIVE EDUCATION · CREATIVE PAPERBACKS

Published by Creative Education and Creative Paperbacks
P.O. Box 227, Mankato, Minnesota 56002
Creative Education and Creative Paperbacks
are imprints of The Creative Company
www.thecreativecompany.us

Design and production by Christine Vanderbeek
Art direction by Rita Marshall
Printed in the United States of America

Photographs by Alamy (B Christopher, Anders Ryman), Corbis (Bettmann, Bowers Museum,
Corbis, Werner Forman, E. O. Hoppe, James S. Southers/Demotix, Tom Till/SuperStock), Getty
Images (Jim Brandenburg, DEA/G. DAGLI ORTI), iStockphoto (aslitoprak, foofie, Grafissimo,
Marilyn Haddrill), Shutterstock (bobby20, Steve Collender, Zack Frank, OHishiapply,
Menno Schaefer, Transia Design), SuperStock (SuperStock)

Library of Congress Cataloging-in-Publication Data
Bodden, Valerie.
Apache / Valerie Bodden.
p. cm. — (Peoples of North America) • Includes bibliographical references and index.
Summary: A history of the people and events that influenced the North American Indian tribe
known as the Apache, including warrior Geronimo and conflicts such as the Camp Grant Massacre.
ISBN 978-1-60818-550-4 (hardcover)
ISBN 978-1-62832-151-7 (pbk)
1. Apache Indians—Juvenile literature. I. Title.

E99.A6B75 2015
979.004'9725—dc23   2014041744

CCSS: RI.5.1, 2, 3, 5, 6, 8, 9; RH.6-8.4, 5, 6, 7, 8, 9

HC 9 8 7 6 5 4 3 2
PBK 9 8 7 6 5 4 3 2

PEOPLES of NORTH AMERICA

Apache

VALERIE BODDEN

CREATIVE EDUCATION · CREATIVE PAPERBACKS

Table of Contents

An Apache family in the 1890s (on page 3);
a modern intertribal powwow in Texas
(pictured here)

APACHE

Introduction

PEOPLES of NORTH AMERICA

For hundreds of years, the American Southwest was known as Apachería—the Spanish name for the homeland of the Apache Indians. It was a land of contrasts. Steep **MESAS** and cliffs rose up from dry, rocky deserts pierced by cacti and yucca. In places, deep canyons chiseled a path through the deserts. Rivers lined with willow and cottonwood roared through the canyons in the spring, but their flow slowed to a dribble at the height of summer. Elsewhere, bison and pronghorn wandered across arid plains that gave way to jagged, snow-capped mountains. The mountainsides grew thick with pine, piñon, and juniper, providing shelter for deer, bears, and turkeys. Moving through this land of extremes with the seasons, the Apache found everything they needed to survive: wild plants to harvest, animals to hunt, and strongholds in which to hide when threatened.

The Apache called themselves *Ndee* or *Tinneh*, meaning "The People." The name "Apache" is likely a Spanish interpretation of the Zuni Indian word *apachu*, or "enemy." Although they were known by one name, the Apache were never united as a single group. Instead, there were several Apache tribes linked by a common language and culture. That culture was threatened as newcomers—first the Spanish and then the Americans—invaded Apachería. But the Apache fought hard to defend their homeland, earning a reputation for being some of the most fearsome Indians in North America. Eventually, though, they were defeated and moved onto reservations, where many continue the fight to retain their culture today.

MESCALERO APACHE LIVED FOR A TIME
NEAR THE CHISOS MOUNTAINS OF TEXAS.

Although the Apache are known as a southwestern tribe, they did not arrive in the Southwest until sometime between A.D. 1000 and 1500. Before that time, the ancestors of the Apache lived in present-day Alaska and western Canada. There they hunted caribou, moose, and bears and made shelters from poles covered with branches or animal hides.

ANTHROPOLOGISTS call these ancestral Apache Athapaskans because the language they spoke belongs to the Athapaskan language family. Many Athapaskan-speaking peoples remained in the north. But at some point, groups of them began to move south, possibly because of food shortages or hostilities waged against neighboring peoples.

Likely traveling in small family groups, the people migrated slowly, possibly over a period of hundreds of years. They probably traveled along the plains east of the Rocky Mountains. When they reached locations where food was plentiful, they may have settled for a time before continuing their southward journey.

Eventually, the groups entered the American Southwest, where they spread out across parts of present-day Arizona, Colorado, New Mexico, Texas, Kansas, and Oklahoma. Some entered northern Mexico. As they

APACHE ANCESTORS MOVED FROM ALASKA'S BROWN-BEAR COUNTRY TO THE WARMER ENVIRONS OF THE SOUTHWEST.

moved into these different regions, the Athapaskans began to break into separate tribes. Each tribe settled in its own geographic area and adopted its own customs and way of life.

One group of Athapaskans, the Navajo, settled in northern New Mexico and adopted a lifestyle so different from the other tribes that they became known as a separate people. The remaining Athapaskans became the Apache. They were divided into six tribes: the Mescalero, Jicarilla (*hee-kuh-REE-ya*), Chiricahua (*chee-ree-KA-wuh*), Lipan, Kiowa-Apache, and Western Apache.

The Mescalero, Jicarilla, Chiricahua, Lipan, and Kiowa-Apache were known as Eastern Apache tribes because they lived in the eastern part of the Apache homeland. Many of these tribes remained for a time on the Great Plains before being pushed south by other Indian peoples such as the Comanche. As a result, they were influenced by the culture of the Plains Indians and relied heavily on bison hunting. Some of the tribes, such as the Jicarilla, also farmed.

To the west, the Western Apache tribe was divided into five subtribes: Northern Tonto, Southern Tonto, Cibecue, White Mountain, and San Carlos. The farming techniques of their **PUEBLOAN** neighbors influenced the Western Apache. Of all the Apache tribes, the Western Apache farmed most extensively.

While some of the Apache tribes and bands regularly interacted with one another, others had very little contact. However, most Apache tribes traded and fought with other Indian peoples. When they first reached the Southwest, the Apache established friendly relationships with the Puebloan peoples who had lived in the region for centuries. They offered animal skins, meat, and salt to the Pueblos in return for foods such as corn and squash, as well as

↦→ **BEST BEHAVIOR** ↤← *Apache parents taught their children to respect and obey their elders. A disobedient child was usually ignored until he behaved. Or his mother might splash his face with cold water. If he continued to act out, his grandfather dressed up like an evil ogre and scared the child while he was sleeping at night. Since the child had heard many times that ogres took naughty children away to their underground lairs, he quickly agreed to behave.*

cotton clothing. Groups of Apache also traded with the Yavapai of western Arizona. And some Apache tribes traveled far into Mexico to sell their goods to natives there in return for turquoise, pottery, and coral.

Sometimes, instead of making deals for what they needed, the Apache raided to steal goods from other peoples. Soon after the Spanish entered the American Southwest in the 1500s, they became a target of Apache raids. The Apache especially wanted Spanish horses and became one of the first Indian groups to acquire them. The horses made it easier for the Apache to travel and hunt bison. The animals also became a valuable new food source. In addition to stealing from the Spanish, the Apache also raided other Indian peoples, such as the Pima, Papago, Maricopa, Havasupai, and Walapai. Even trade partners such as the Pueblos were not safe from Apache raiders. On the Plains, the Apache clashed with the Pawnee.

Their lifestyle of hunting, gathering, and raiding required the Apache to move frequently. As a result, they needed homes that could be set up and taken down—or abandoned—quickly. Most Apache lived in wickiups. These dome-shaped structures were

HERBAL REMEDIES *Although the Apache relied on ceremonies to cure illnesses believed to be caused by evil spirits, they used natural remedies for other sicknesses. To treat an earache, otter grease was rubbed in the ear. A cough was cured with a robin's egg mixed in water, while facial blemishes were covered with a lotion made of ground moss and mushrooms. Fear—also considered an illness—could be cured by a drink brewed from herbs mixed with the brain and eye of a woodhouse jay.*

made from a frame of poles covered with brush, grass, or yucca leaves. In the winter, animal skins might cover the wickiup to provide more warmth. Most wickiups were about 10 to 12 feet (3–3.7 m) across and stood 7 to 9 feet (2.1–2.7 m) high in the center. An opening in the eastern side of the wickiup served as a door. Inside, the wickiup might be furnished with wooden beds raised two or three feet (0.6–0.9 m) off the ground—and little else. When the Apache moved to a new campsite, they left their wickiup behind and built a new one in their new location.

Instead of a wickiup, the Lipan, Kiowa-Apache, Mescalero, and some Jicarilla generally lived in Plains-style tepees. Other Apache tribes may have used tepees on occasion as well. The tepees were erected by arranging long poles into a cone shape and covering them with bison hides. Most tepees were about 14 feet (4.3 m) across. They were easy to set up and take down—ideal for bison hunters who moved camps often. The poles and covering could even be used to make a **TRAVOIS** for carrying a family's possessions from camp to camp.

In addition to their wickiup or tepee, most Apache families also built a ramada to provide shade during the intense heat of

THE CEREMONIAL CLOTHING OF AN APACHE BRIDE (ABOVE) DIFFERED FROM THAT OF EVERYDAY WEAR (RIGHT).

summer. The rectangular-shaped ramada consisted of four support poles topped by a roof of brush or grass. A ramada generally had no walls. Women might gather there to cook or complete other tasks.

Most Apache set up their homes in extended family groups centered on the oldest woman in the family. The woman and her husband lived in one dwelling. Their unmarried adult children lived nearby, as did their married daughters, with their own families.

The various extended families in an area joined together to form a local group. The local group was generally made up of anywhere from 2 to 20 extended families, giving it a population between 35 and 200. Usually, the members of a local group were related by blood or marriage or had close friendship ties. The families of the local group camped, hunted, gathered wild plants, raided, and held ceremonies together.

Among some tribes, all the local groups in a specific region were recognized as a band. The Jicarilla, for example, were divided into two bands. The Llanero band adopted a Plains lifestyle, while the Ollero band took up pottery making learned from the Pueblo. The Chiricahua tribe was divided into three bands: Eastern (also known as Mimbreño), Central, and Southern. Most bands had 50 to 750 members, and each band generally lived and hunted in its own territory.

As they moved across Apachería, setting up their homes and camps, the Apache considered themselves to be a living part of the land. It provided them with food and shelter, and they believed it had been created just for them. As the famous Apache warrior Geronimo explained: "Thus it was in the beginning: the Apaches and their homes, each created for the other."

· APACHE ·

Life on the Move

— PEOPLES *of* NORTH AMERICA —

lthough they shared a common culture and language, the Apache were never united as a single group under one leader. The separate Apache tribes did not form their own centralized governments, either; there was no head chief of the Jicarilla or the Chiricahua or any other tribe. Instead, the various bands and local groups of each tribe operated independently.

Each local group was led by a chief chosen for his experience, wisdom, and generosity. The position of chief was not necessarily hereditary, but the son of a chief often took up the position after his father died. The chief led discussions, and his advice carried weight with his people, but he ruled by **CONSENSUS**. Any family that disagreed with a chief's decisions was free to ignore them or to join a different local group.

Each band elected its own principal chief—often the strongest leader from among the local group chiefs. Like the local chief, the band chief ruled by consensus, with no authority to enforce his decisions. At times, two or more bands might join together to wage war on a common enemy. In those cases, a separate war leader might be chosen, but the bands and local groups were free to follow their own leaders. When the conflict was over, the bands separated.

A MEMBER OF THE CHIRICAHUA TRIBE, CHATTO
RAIDED SETTLERS BEFORE ACTING AS AN ARMY
SCOUT IN THE 1870S.

ONCE SETTLERS
BEGAN MOVING
INTO MORE APACHE
LANDS, RAIDING
PARTIES TARGETED
THEIR HOMES, TOO.

The Apache distinguished between two types of conflict: raids and warfare. Raids were conducted to obtain needed supplies such as food and horses, while wars were waged to avenge Apache deaths. Most raiding parties were small, consisting of 5 to 10 men, although at times they numbered 50 or more. Raiders approached their target on horseback or on foot under the cover of darkness. Then, in the early morning hours, they sneaked up to the enemy's horse herd and drove the animals home, often traveling without rest for several days. In addition to horses, the Apache also raided for clothing, blankets, saddles, guns, sheep, and cattle.

While the goal of a raid was to plunder the enemy without engaging in battle, the goal of a war was to kill as many of the enemy as possible. Apache war parties were generally much larger than raiding parties, and before they left camp, a war dance was held to ensure success. Battles were often fought in the early-morning hours. Warriors carried a bow and arrows, war clubs, lances, knives, and—later—guns. Some used bison- or cowhide shields.

The Apache moved through their land according to the seasons. In the spring, those tribes that farmed planted their crops of corn, beans, and squash near water sources. But these crops provided only a small part of their diet. Most of the Apaches' food came from wild plants and animals. Once the fields were planted, they were either left alone or looked after by the elderly or young. Meanwhile, the rest of the tribe gathered wild plants.

In early spring, the desert plants began to bloom. Among the most important of these plants was mescal, a staple in the diet

⤝ **GERONIMO** ⤜ *Geronimo was born in 1829 in northern Mexico. Although not a chief, Geronimo was a* **SHAMAN** *and a strong warrior who fought under leaders such as Cochise. In 1858, his wife and children were killed by Mexican soldiers. Afterward, Geronimo led numerous bloody raids into Mexico to avenge their deaths. Beginning in 1876, he led small bands against American forces intent on moving the Apache onto reservations. In 1886, Geronimo surrendered, an act he regretted for the rest of his life. He died of pneumonia in 1909.*

of many tribes. As spring turned to summer, the Apache generally headed into the mountains to harvest additional wild plants. Among the wild foods Apachería provided its people were yucca, cactus fruits, acorns, juniper berries, wild onions, chokecherries, and mulberries.

In the fall, the Apache returned to harvest their crops before continuing to gather wild foods such as piñon nuts. As women handled farming and gathering, men prepared for the hunt. Before embarking on a hunt, they participated in special ceremonies. Hunters generally worked alone or in small groups. A hunter's main weapon was the bow and arrow, which he used to take deer, pronghorn, elk, mountain sheep, and turkey. Sometimes hunters wore a deer or pronghorn mask to sneak up on game. Other times, they chased their prey to the point of exhaustion and then caught it with a rope. Some tribes took part in large-scale bison hunts on the Plains. Such hunts might last more than two weeks and involve hunters from several bands. Much of the meat was dried and stored for winter use.

In the winter, the Apache set up semi-permanent camps in river valleys, where the weather was milder than in the mountains. Men continued to hunt and went on raids when food supplies got low. Women spent the winter tanning animal skins, making clothing, and weaving baskets from plants such as yucca, sumac, and mulberry. Some of the baskets were up to four feet (1.2 m) tall and could be used to store food or to carry firewood. They often had a strap that could be tied around the top of a woman's head so that the basket would hang down her back. A watertight seal made from piñon **PITCH** coated baskets used to carry water. Apache baskets became valuable trade items among not only other Indian tribes but also the Americans who began to enter the area in the 1800s.

LIKE THEIR PLAINS NEIGHBORS, THE APACHE WHO HUNTED BISON DEPENDED ON THE ANIMAL FOR MEAT AND MATERIALS.

In addition to finding and preparing foods and making baskets, Apache women cared for the children. Infants were placed in a **CRADLEBOARD** for their first several months. Around the age of 9 or 10, children began to help their parents around the camp. Girls learned to gather food, construct wickiups, and cook. Boys helped their fathers make weapons and even made their own small bows and arrows to use for practice. But boys were not allowed to participate in hunts or warfare until they were closer to age 16. Even then, during his first expeditions, the boy was tasked with certain jobs. He collected firewood, cared for the warriors' horses, and stood guard at camp but did not participate in the fighting. After four training expeditions, the boy "arrived at the point where he [was] a real man," according to one Chiricahua warrior.

While boys became men through warfare, girls became women through a special ceremony known as the Sunrise Dance. This four-day and four-night ceremony was held when a girl entered **PUBERTY**. During the Sunrise Dance, she wore a yellow buckskin

dress, was sprinkled with pollen, and participated in special dances. After the ceremony, the girl could be married.

During the Sunrise Dance, the girl was believed to represent Changing Woman (also known as White Painted Woman), one of the main Apache gods. Other gods included Killer of Enemies, Child Born of Water, and Yusn, the creator of the universe. The *gaan* were mountain spirits who could be called upon in special ceremonies to help human beings. In the Apache tradition, everything in the universe was thought to have spiritual power.

Men and women who were believed to have especially strong spiritual powers became shamans, or medicine people. Some shamans served as healers, while others were believed to control the weather. Shamans also directed the people in carrying out ceremonies to cure or prevent illness or misfortune. Such ceremonies often lasted several nights and might involve up to 80 different songs and chants, along with dances.

CEREMONIAL SINGING ACCOMPANIES THE APACHE SUNRISE DANCE, EVEN TODAY.

· APACHE ·

Violent Encounters

PEOPLES *of* NORTH AMERICA

In the 1520s, Spanish explorers began to march through present-day Mexico, claiming the land for Spain. Soon, they forged north into the American Southwest. In 1541, an expedition led by Francisco Vásquez de Coronado entered the region. His was the first documented encounter with the Apache, whom he reported were "gentle people, faithful in their friendships."

By 1598, Spain had laid claim to New Mexico, and settlers began to arrive in the region. The Apache traded with the newcomers, providing them with animal skins in return for tools and horses. Often, though, the Apache obtained their horses by raiding the Spanish herds. They also acquired guns through raids, but these weapons did them little good without gunpowder and lead, and guns were not widely used by the Apache until the mid-1800s.

Even as the Apache raided the Spanish for horses, the Spanish also raided the Apache—for people, whom they sold as slaves. By 1627, tensions between the Apache and the Spanish had escalated into all-out warfare, which would continue for more than 150 years. During this period, the Apache repeatedly launched attacks on Spanish supply trains, ranches, and towns. From 1748 to 1770 alone, they killed more than 4,000 soldiers and settlers. For their part,

WITH HORSES, AMERICAN INDIANS COULD TRAVEL
FARTHER AND FASTER, BUT THEY ALSO FACED
GREATER CONFLICT.

the Spanish built forts and sent out troops against the Apache. But there was little they could do to stop the Indians, who disappeared into mountain strongholds whenever they were attacked.

Beginning in 1786, the Spanish government decided to try a new tactic. Spanish armies continued to launch attacks on the raiding Apache, but they also offered food and protection to any Apache who surrendered. Many Apache agreed to the terms and went to live near the Spanish forts. In addition to food, they were given guns and liquor. The guns were old and in poor condition, guaranteeing their ineffective use as weapons. And the liquor was intended to keep the Apache subdued and unable to fight. The plan worked to some extent, and there was a degree of peace. But it cost the Spanish government $18,000 to $30,000 a year.

AFTER TEXAS BECAME A STATE IN 1845, MEXICO STILL LAID CLAIM TO THE TERRITORY AND FOUGHT AGAINST THE U.S.

In 1821, Mexico gained independence from Spain. The Mexican government could not afford to supply the Apache with food, guns, and liquor, and the Apache quickly resumed their raiding practices. By 1836, they had killed another 5,000-some settlers. Thousands more had left the area, abandoning entire settlements. As a result, the Mexican states of Sonora and Chihuahua began to offer a reward for Apache **SCALPS**: $100 for a male's scalp, $50 for a female's, and $25 for a child's. Soon, bounty hunters from both Mexico and America were turning over hundreds of scalps in return for payment.

In 1848, much of the Southwest passed into the hands of the United States at the end of the **MEXICAN-AMERICAN WAR**. The new border between the U.S. and Mexico ran through Apachería. At first, the Apache welcomed the Americans, who had defeated their

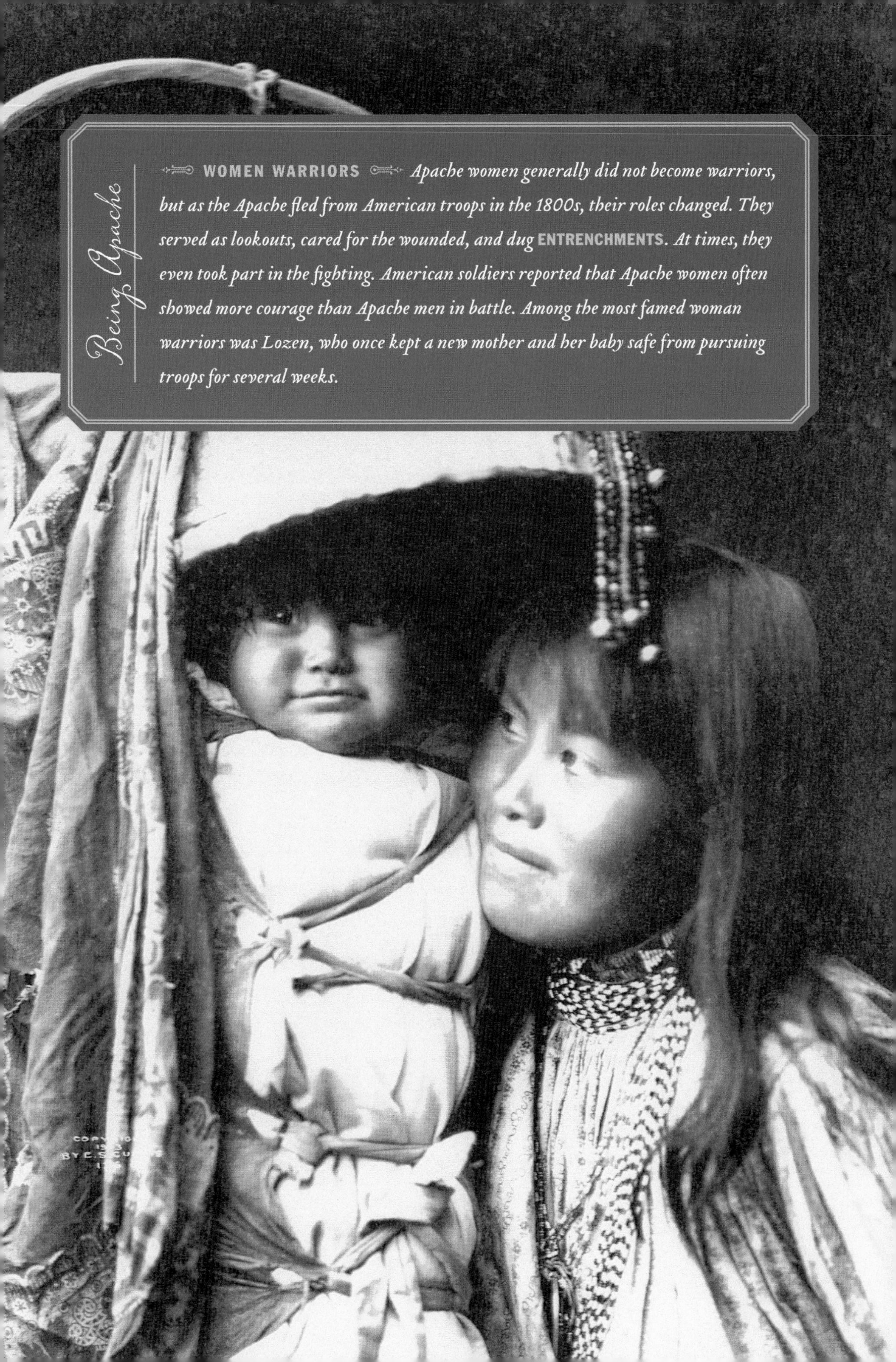

WOMEN WARRIORS ✦ *Apache women generally did not become warriors, but as the Apache fled from American troops in the 1800s, their roles changed. They served as lookouts, cared for the wounded, and dug* ENTRENCHMENTS. *At times, they even took part in the fighting. American soldiers reported that Apache women often showed more courage than Apache men in battle. Among the most famed woman warriors was Lozen, who once kept a new mother and her baby safe from pursuing troops for several weeks.*

COPYRIGHT
BY C.S.CU
1

traditional enemy, the Mexicans. But the American government demanded that the Apache stop all raids, even those in Mexico. Apache leaders told U.S. officials this was not possible, since raids provided needed food. "We must steal from somebody; and if you will not permit us to rob the Mexicans, we must steal from you or fight you," a group of Mescalero chiefs announced.

As Apachería filled with Americans traveling west to California, where gold was discovered in early 1848, Apache bands took aim at the travelers, killing hundreds. With Apache raiders seeming to attack everywhere at once, settlers and soldiers assumed their population to be close to 30,000. Historians now say the true figure was probably 6,000 to 8,000. Though American troops patrolled the area and engaged the Apache in numerous battles, they could not bring the attacks under control. Whenever troops closed in, the Apache slipped across the border into Mexico, where they had learned the American soldiers couldn't follow.

Occasionally, tribes such as the Jicarilla and the Mescalero sought peace with the Americans. Although they signed treaties, those agreements were never **RATIFIED** by the U.S. Senate. When the government failed to deliver the food and protection promised

APACHE SCOUTS *Apache scouts often joined the U.S. Army on its missions against other Apache. In many cases, the scouts belonged to different tribes or bands than those being pursued—and sometimes they weren't on friendly terms. Scouts were provided with knives and guns. Some were given only a small amount of ammunition—since it was their job to find the enemy Apache, not to fight them. They wore red turbans so that the soldiers could tell them apart from the warriors.*

by the treaties, the Apache started raiding again.

In 1858, the Chiricahua made a peace agreement with the Americans. It lasted three years. But in 1861, an army lieutenant named George Bascom invited the Chiricahua chief Cochise into his tent. Bascom accused Cochise of kidnapping a young American boy and stealing cattle. When Cochise denied the charge, Bascom's soldiers surrounded him. Cochise slashed through the tent wall and escaped, but six of his men were captured and executed. As Cochise later explained, the soldiers "did me a very great wrong, and I and my people went to war with them." Within 2 months, 150 Americans in Apachería had been killed in retaliation. For the next 10 years, the Chiricahua—led by Cochise—launched almost constant attacks against the Americans.

Meanwhile, General James H. Carleton, commander of the army's southwestern forces, decided the Mescalero Apache should be placed on a reservation in New Mexico. In 1862, he enlisted famed frontiersman **CHRISTOPHER "KIT" CARSON** to force them to move. "All Indian men of that tribe are to be killed whenever and wherever you can find them," Carleton ordered. "The women and children will not be harmed, but you will take them prisoners."

Although the Mescalero attempted to hide, they were eventually rounded up and forcibly led to the Bosque Redondo reservation. There the nearly 500 Mescalero were joined by more than 9,000 Navajo. After four years of suffering from disease and hunger on the reservation, the Mescalero made their escape into the mountains.

By now, the government had begun to construct forts throughout Apachería. Many Western Apache agreed to settle near these forts and live at peace with the Americans. Some even joined American forces as scouts against other Apache groups. One Western Apache band, called the Aravaipa, settled near Camp Grant in Arizona. On April 30, 1871, a group of Arizona settlers rode into the Aravaipa camp and killed more than 125 of its inhabitants, mostly women and children.

The Camp Grant Massacre, as it was known, spurred president Ulysses S. Grant to lay out his Peace Policy. The policy would move all Apache onto reservations in order to "promote peace and civilization among them." Four reservations were established throughout Apachería, and within weeks, more than 4,000 Apache had agreed to move onto them.

Others, such as Cochise, continued to fight. But by September 1872, even he was ready to give in. He was promised that his people could remain on a reservation in their own lands. But he admitted to the officials negotiating the treaty that he didn't think they would honor the agreement. He gave them a warning: "If you try to move us again, war will start once more; it will be a war without end, a war in which every Apache will fight until he is dead." The warning fell on deaf ears.

As Cochise and his people settled onto their unofficial reservation (the treaty creating it hadn't been ratified by the Senate), other Apache bands continued to resist moving onto reservations. The government launched campaigns against them until, one by one, they surrendered. By the end of 1873, most Apache bands had been contained on reservations, but from time to time, various bands escaped and conducted raids. Although the different Apache tribes had at first been settled on separate reservations, in 1874, the government began moving them onto the San Carlos Reservation in southeastern Arizona.

That same year, Cochise died of illness. Two years later, the government broke its promise to allow his people to remain on their land. In June 1876, the Chiricahua were ordered to relocate to San Carlos. Although 325 Chiricahua agreed to go, another 600 or more fled into the mountains of Mexico under the leadership of strong warriors such as Geronimo, Juh, and Victorio. Those who fled knew their chances of survival were small. "All of us knew that we were doomed," Geronimo's nephew Daklugie said, "but some preferred death to slavery and imprisonment."

By July, the Chiricahua renegades were crossing the border into the U.S. to launch attacks. Between raids, they sometimes found shelter on the Warm

FOR MANY YEARS, GERONIMO'S FIGHTING SPIRIT
WAS MOTIVATED BY THE 1858 KILLING OF HIS FAMILY.

GERONIMO AND HIS
BAND OF WARRIORS
DID NOT GIVE IN
EASILY, AND THEIR
EXPLOITS BECAME
LEGENDARY.

Springs Reservation, which was home to many Mescalero Apache who had come out of hiding after fleeing Bosque Redondo. While he was at Warm Springs in 1877, Geronimo was surrounded and captured by American troops. He and all the Apache at Warm Springs were led on a forced march to San Carlos. Although he escaped the next year, Geronimo surrendered in 1879 and was again taken to the reservation.

While other bands continued to fight, Geronimo and his people remained at peace for a time. But conditions at San Carlos soon proved intolerable. Corrupt Indian agents (people who were supposed to deal with the Indians on the government's behalf) sold off the food and other supplies the government was supposed to provide to the Apache, who often went hungry. Heat and pests made life miserable, too. "Take stones and ashes and thorns and, with some scorpions and rattlesnakes thrown in, dump the outfit on stones, heat the stones red-hot, and set the United States Army after the Apaches, and you have San Carlos," Daklugie said.

In 1881, Geronimo, Juh, and other warriors led 700 Apache men, women, and children to escape from the reservation into the mountains of Mexico. The U.S. Army again pursued them. Two years later, General George Crook took a small company of soldiers, along with nearly 200 Apache scouts, into Mexico. When

⟿ TRAVELING LIGHT ⟾ *While American troops were slowed by pack wagons loaded with food, water, ammunition, and other supplies, the Apache carried only the necessities. Belts wrapped around the body held ammunition. For food, a warrior took only some dried meat and roasted mescal. He obtained the rest of his food from the land—from wild plants to small game. If his horse died, it made a meal as well. Its intestines could even be cleaned to hold enough water to last the family a week.*

the scouts located Geronimo, he agreed to surrender.

But by 1885, Geronimo was once again disgusted with life at San Carlos. He escaped back to Mexico with 42 warriors and 92 women and children. From their stronghold, the small band of Apache continued to launch raids into the U.S. The army finally caught up with them in March 1886. Geronimo again agreed to surrender, but fearing his people would be killed, he escaped once more, this time with 39 men, women, and children.

A force of 5,000 American troops, plus 3,000 Mexican volunteers, a civilian **MILITIA**, and 500 Apache scouts, combed the mountains looking for Geronimo's group. After six months, Apache scouts located the hideout. On September 4, 1886, Geronimo surrendered without a fight. "Once I moved about like the wind," he said. "Now I surrender to you and that is all." The last Apache had been subdued.

Afterward, all the Chiricahua—including the scouts who had helped capture Geronimo and those who had been settled peacefully at San Carlos—were sent to prison camps in Florida. More than 100 died there. Geronimo had been promised that after two years of imprisonment, his people could return to their land. But in 1888, the Chiricahua were transferred to a prison camp in Alabama, where many contracted **TUBERCULOSIS** and **MALARIA**.

After six years in Alabama, the Chiricahua were finally freed from their prison in 1894. But they still weren't taken home. Instead, they were placed on a reservation at Fort Sill in present-day Oklahoma. Although it wasn't home, the Chiricahua were grateful to be able to see mountains and sky again. They began to farm and raise cattle.

In 1913, 27 years after they had been taken from their homeland, the Chiricahua were finally released from the reservation. They were given the choice of remaining on a land **ALLOTMENT**

THE CAPTURED
APACHE PRISONERS
WERE TRANSPORTED
BY RAILWAY TO FLOR-
IDA BY WAY OF SAN
ANTONIO, TEXAS.

in Oklahoma or settling on the Mescalero Reservation in New Mexico. Of the 1,675 Chiricahua who had lived in Apachería in 1873, only 258 survived. Nearly 90 of them chose to remain in Oklahoma. They became known as the Fort Sill Apache. The rest moved to the Mescalero Reservation.

Even as the Chiricahua had been suffering through their imprisonment and exile, life on the Mescalero and other Apache reservations hadn't been easy. On most reservations, the Apache were expected to adopt American lifestyles. They were forced to cut their hair and wear American-style clothing. Traditional ceremonies were forbidden. Children were shipped to boarding schools, where many died of diseases brought to North America by the Europeans.

By the 1930s, life on the reservations had begun to improve somewhat. Industries such as cattle raising and lumber sales brought new sources of income. Children were allowed to attend day schools instead of boarding schools, and health programs were set up on the reservations.

Today, more than 100,000 people in the U.S. claim Apache descent. Many of them continue to live on reservations in New Mexico and Arizona. Some members of the Fort Sill Apache

> **⟿ FIGHT FOR MOUNT GRAHAM ⟾** *In 1989, the University of Arizona began constructing an observatory on Arizona's Mount Graham despite Apache protests. The mountain has long been a sacred site for the Apache, who believe it is the home of the gaan mountain spirits. Apache ceremonies featuring gaan dancers were once held on the mountain, which also contains many Apache burial sites. Today, the Mount Graham International Observatory hosts one of the world's largest telescopes. The Apache continue to protest the disrespectful use of their sacred peak.*

remain in Oklahoma. Other Apache live in various places around the world. Unemployment is high on the Apache reservations, but casinos, resorts, and other tourist attractions have brought new opportunities for income in recent years.

Many Apache today continue to practice elements of their traditional culture. The Sunrise Dance is still celebrated by many young girls to mark their transition to womanhood. Some Apache still take part in healing ceremonies as well. The Apache language continues to be spoken by some, and classes in the language are offered at reservation schools. Apache women still make and sell baskets, too.

The Apache know that these traditions are not only a part of their past but also of their future. "If Apaches are going to be here in 200 years—and be Apache—they're going to need to maintain both worlds…. If they don't, the world will just absorb us," said Wesley Bonito, an Apache tribal educator, in the late 20th century. The Apache way of life has changed much in the past 1,000 years. From their early days in the far north to their clashes with Mexican and American forces in Apachería and their relocation onto reservations, the Apache have adjusted to the demands of a changing world while fiercely protecting their traditions.

PARTICIPANTS IN TRADITIONAL APACHE CELEBRATIONS MAKE THEMSELVES HEARD IN A CROWD, THANKS TO MICROPHONES.

As they settled into their winter camps, the Apache spent the long nights listening to the older men and women tell stories. These stories taught lessons and explained the world in which the Apache lived. In this story told by the Jicarilla Apache, a young hero saves his people from the Giant Elk and Giant Eagle. In the process, mountains are made and animals develop certain characteristics.

Long ago, giant animals and birds attacked and ate people. The worst were Elk and Eagle. One day, Jonayaíyin, a child of Sun, was sent to save the people. Jonayaíyin asked his mother where Elk lived. She told him to go to the great desert in the south. Jonayaíyin took four steps and was there.

He hid behind a hill to watch Elk on the open plains. He could not figure out a way to sneak up on Elk, since there were no trees to hide behind. Just then, Lizard came to him and asked what he was doing. When Jonayaíyin told him, Lizard said the boy should disguise himself in the skin of a lizard. So Jonayaíyin did.

Then Gopher stopped to ask what Jonayaíyin was doing. When Jonayaíyin told him, Gopher suggested that he burrow under the ground to reach Elk. Then Gopher began to dig a long tunnel for Jonayaíyin. He stopped when he got to Elk and poked his head out of the tunnel. He began to gnaw off the hair around Elk's giant heart. He told Elk he needed the hair to keep his children warm. So Elk let him keep gnawing. Soon, Elk's magic coat had been cut away from all around his heart.

When Gopher returned to Jonayaíyin, the boy made his way through the tunnel. He shot four arrows into Elk's heart. Then he fled back through the tunnel, but Elk stuck his antler into the tunnel and followed the boy. As he chased Jonayaíyin, Elk's antlers threw up huge chunks of earth, raising up mountains that extended from east to west. At the end of the tunnel, Elk ran into a web made by Black Spider, so he turned south, throwing up more mountains. Finally, Elk was too injured to go on, and he fell down dead. Jonayaíyin made a coat from his hide and gave the meat to Gopher and Lizard. He carried the antlers with him.

After killing Elk, Jonayaíyin decided to go after Eagle. He took four steps to the west and reached Eagle's homeland. Then he stood waiting for Eagle to swoop down and pick him up. At last Eagle did. She carried him to her nest and dropped him in it to feed her children. But Jonayaíyin was still alive, and he kept the young eagles from eating him. When their mother and father returned to the nest, he killed them with Elk's antlers. Then he hit the young eagles on the head so they would never grow any larger.

But now Jonayaíyin was stuck in Eagle's nest on a high rock. He asked Bat to help him down. In return, he promised to give her feathers. So Bat flew Jonayaíyin to the ground in a basket hanging from a thread of spider silk. Then Jonayaíyin filled the basket with feathers. But he warned Bat not to take her feathers onto the plains, where the little birds would steal them. Bat went to the plains anyway, and the little birds stole the feathers. Four times Jonayaíyin gave her more feathers, but each time they were taken away by little birds. Finally, Jonayaíyin told Bat that since she couldn't take care of her feathers, she would never have any. And she has none to this day.

ALLOTMENT
a portion set aside for an individual;
many American Indians were forced to
take allotments from tribal lands, with
any remaining lands going to the U.S.
government

ANTHROPOLOGISTS
people who study the physical traits,
cultures, and relationships of different
peoples

CHRISTOPHER "KIT" CARSON
(1809–68) American explorer who guided
military expeditions to the western U.S.;
he served as an Indian agent to the Ute and
in 1862 led the roundup of the Mescalero
Apache to send them to Bosque Redondo

CONSENSUS
agreement by all or most of a group

CRADLEBOARD
a board or frame to which an infant could
be strapped to be carried on the back

ENTRENCHMENTS
ditches or holes that offer a strong defensive
position against attackers

MALARIA
a disease that causes chills, fever, and
often death and is spread to humans by
mosquitoes

MESAS
flat, raised areas of land with steep sides

MEXICAN–AMERICAN WAR
fought from 1846 to 1848 between the
U.S. and Mexico over Texas, the conflict
resulted in the U.S. gaining control over the
lands of the American Southwest

MILITIA
an army made up of citizens instead of
professional soldiers

PITCH
a sticky substance made from the sap of
evergreen trees

PUBERTY
the stage of development during which
boys and girls become physically able to
reproduce

PUEBLOAN
having to do with the Pueblo Indians, who
lived in the American Southwest in large,
flat-roofed housing complexes

RATIFIED
made an agreement official by voting for or
signing it

SCALPS
portions of the skin at the top of the head,
with the attached hair, that were sometimes
cut off of enemies as battle trophies or to
claim a reward

SHAMAN
a spiritual leader often believed to have
healing and other powers

TRAVOIS
a vehicle made of two poles crossed into a
V-shape at one end, with a bison hide hung
between them to serve as a platform; the
travois was hitched to a dog or horse, with
the ends dragging on the ground

TUBERCULOSIS
a contagious disease that causes fever,
cough, and difficulty breathing

Hoxie, Frederick E., ed. *Encyclopedia of North American Indians*. Boston: Houghton Mifflin, 1996.

Josephy, Alvin M. Jr. *500 Nations: An Illustrated History of North American Indians*. New York: Knopf, 1994.

Kehoe, Alice B. *North American Indians: A Comprehensive Account*. 2nd ed. Englewood Cliffs, N.J.: Prentice Hall, 1992.

Mails, Thomas E. *The People Called Apache*. New York: Promontory Press, 1981.

Reedstrom, E. Lisle. *Apache Wars: An Illustrated Battle History*. New York: Sterling, 1990.

Terrell, John Upton. *Apache Chronicle: The Story of the People*. New York: World Publishing, 1972.

Time-Life Editors. *People of the Desert*. Alexandria, Va.: Time-Life Books, 1993.

Trimble, Stephen. *The People: Indians of the American Southwest*. Santa Fe, N. Mex.: School of American Research, 1993.

≈══ READ MORE ══≈

Ake, Anne. *The Apache*. San Diego: Lucent, 2001.

Casey, Carolyn. *The Apache*. New York: Marshall Cavendish Benchmark, 2006.

≈══ WEBSITES ══≈

THE LIPAN APACHE TRIBE OF TEXAS: MUSEUM
http://www.lipanapache.org/Museum /museum.html
Learn more about the Lipan Apache—from their history and famous chiefs to their culture and everyday life.

PURPLE HAWK'S APACHE PHOTO GALLERY
http://www.impurplehawk.com/apgallery.html
Check out historic photos of Apache families, sites, and ceremonies.